CHELTENHAM IN PICTURES

The Promenade, looking north towards High Street. The statue is that of a famous man who was born at Cheltenham and who was educated at the College. He was Edward Adrian Wilson—scientist, doctor and artist—who died in the Antarctic with Captain Scott. Very fittingly, it is by Scott's widow, the sculptress Lady Kennet

CHELTENHAM IN PICTURES

By Bryan Little

1913 — 1992

DAVID & CHARLES : NEWTON ABBOT

7153 4178 2

Printed in Great Britain
by W J Holman Limited Dawlish
for David & Charles (Publishers) Limited
Newton Abbot Devon

A LIST OF MAIN CONTENTS

Pittville; the Pump Room, by John Forbes, 1825-30

An Introductory Sketch

As one promenades along Cheltenham's wide, tree-lined streets, admiring the town's impeccable 'Regency' and 'Grecian' terraces, one thinks of Cheltenham in terms of the architectural achievement of the first few decades of last century. It is, to an overwhelming degree, a town of man-made beauty, unlike Bath in that it owes little of its outstanding quality to the original nature of a site amid the last undulations of central Gloucestershire's plain before it reaches the grander Cotswold scene. One rightly admires the efforts of Cheltenham's planners, planters, and architects in their creation of so admirable a town. Yet behind their endeavours, as a social background to Cheltenham's many humble streets and as an explanation of its more stately districts, one had the varied human picture of the people whose leisure, and whose toil, created both its present appearance and the aspects of its life which have passed into the historic past. Regency bucks and the retired servants of 'John Company', and those who have pursued such callings as those of the tobacco farmer, the flyman, the gas stoker, the coach builder, and the muffin man, all these have combined to make the human blend of the 'Garden Town'.

Some modern spa towns, and many seaside resorts, have risen from insignificance, or even from nullity; one has but to think of Tunbridge Wells and Leamington, of Bournemouth and Blackpool. This is not true of Cheltenham. Mediaeval Cheltenham, and the considerable township which existed in Tudor and Stuart times, was no paltry hamlet but a settlement whose size lay between that of a large village and a small town. Its long street, now the High Street with its busy shops and choking traffic, was the sole important highway of a mediaeval village. It still determines the layout, and the human dispositions, of the modern town. It was long a social chasm, sharply parting the 'artisan' quarter from the large southern reaches wherein it was more 'done' to live. So effective was it as a frontier of gentility that it had much to do with the frustration of Pittville; its barrier status has not wholly lost its force. None of its house fronts are still evidently mediaeval, or even Tudor or Jacobean. But if one looks carefully above the shop fronts of, say, the Saxone and Lennard shoe shops one sees features, of early and middle Georgian character, which take us back to the time when Cheltenham's rise as a spa had indeed commenced but when its massive architectural expansion had yet to get under way. Then a little south of the street one has the charming, tautly-enclosed churchyard, and in its midst the ancient parish church with its eloquent proof of mediaeval Cheltenham as a village above the mid-Gloucestershire average of the centuries before the building of the county's great 'wool' churches. Its windows of the fourteenth century, in the most flowing 'Decorated' style or from the phase of transition between 'Decorated' and 'Perpendicular' Gothic, are notable by any English standards. But most of its monuments were crowded in when Cheltenham was commencing its heyday as a resort, and when its residents were decisively swelled by the retired military, naval, and civil servants of the Honourable East India Company.

The middle Tudor years saw great changes in the manorial lordship of Cheltenham, and in the patronage of St Mary's church, long held by the great Augustinian abbey at Cirencester. But religious upheavals, and the lordship of the Dutton family which started (by purchase) in 1628 caused little change in the appearance of the small town, already possessed of a market and beginning to be of some note for its malting and brewing. We find, from the occupational record of Gloucestershire made by John Smith of Nibley in 1608, that the county's great pursuit of clothmaking was of little importance in Jacobean Cheltenham. Farming, and soon tobacco growing in the area between Cheltenham and Winchcombe, were more important, and the number of Cheltenham's tailors, glovers, and shoemakers suggests a country town whose craftsmen served more customers than those of their own parish.

More important still, for Cheltenham's standing among the rural communities of central Gloucestershire, was its possession of a Grammar School. This school, after a probable gap of some twenty years, had continued one kept by the priest who served a chantry in St Mary's church. Early in the 1570s it was refounded. Richard Pate, a lawyer and a man of note in Gloucestershire who had been among the Commissioners who disposed of the chantries' property, was the timely benefactor. He had studied at Corpus Christi College, Oxford; not long before he died he gave his old college control of the school which was long alone in giving 'secondary' education to Cheltenham boys.

When in 1712 Sir Robert Atkyns's *Ancient and Present State of Gloucestershire* came out, Cheltenham had some 1,500 people. It was a market town and had a considerable malting trade. It stood on the eve of the revelation of its mineral springs. But when in 1716 those mineral waters were discovered some years had yet to pass before Cheltenham's new status much affected all aspects of its life and of its physical appearance. Malting continued, and in 1760 the starting of the 'Original' brewery made a link, still persisting, with the older, agricultural traditions of the district. So too, in St Mary's churchyard, does the headstone to John Higgs, a local stalwart who died in 1825 and whose delight, 'both morning, afternoon, and night', was his far-famed occupation of killing pigs. The spa's first buildings were modest, and as Cheltenham (unlike Bath) was a summer resort ample provision was made for outdoor sauntering. So an early feature of Cheltenham, setting a delightful precedent for its tree-lined walks and roads, was Well Walk, running down from the original well, across the modest stream of the Chelt, and ending its vista with the tower and spire of the parish church. This piece of formal planning was laid out in the 1740s, under the advice of Norborne Berkeley (later Baron Botetourt), that cultivated Gloucestershire magnate whose career ended with the Lord Lieutenancy of his county, and later with the Governorship of Virginia.

The wife of the Manxman, Henry Skillicorne, the retired captain of Bristol merchantmen, inherited the Cheltenham well from her father, William Mason, and in 1738 Skillicorne fenced it in and built a simple canopy to cover the water drinkers. Many more people of rank and fashion visited Cheltenham, with Handel and John Wesley among those who came with a serious professional purpose. Yet in time the boom eased, with travel difficult and a severe lack of good lodgings in a resort which had yet to emulate Bath in a great programme of architectural expansion. Cheltenham's first Master of Ceremonies was, however, appointed in 1780, and in 1784 the town's first Assembly Rooms were opened in the High Street. The building was of modest size but of considerable elegance, perhaps by Henry Holland, the favoured architect of high Whig society. In four years more Cheltenham got the shot in the arm which decided its future and was of some note for the whole social relationship between Throne and People.

In the summer of 1788 George III did for the little Gloucestershire spa what no reigning Hanoverian monarch ever did for Bath—he paid it a personal visit, staying for some weeks. At once, and for years to come, he made Cheltenham the most fashionable spa. His tastes were simple, and court life at Cheltenham was on the modest scale congenial to 'Farmer George'. But his mere presence brought throngs of fashionable visitors, and the whole 'Cheltenham episode' was well chronicled, from her presence there as a lady-in-waiting to Queen Charlotte, by Fanny Burney the novelist. One noted the easy informality of the King's strolls along Well Walk, his friendly contacts with humble local folk, and his visits to such places as Cotswold cloth mills, the Three Choirs Festival at Worcester, and the classical eastern entrance to the new Sapperton tunnel on the Thames & Severn Canal. William III, Queen Anne, and the first two Hanoverian sovereigns had confined themselves to the London area, or in the case of the three kings had split their time between England and their other dominions across the North Sea. They had been remote from many of their English subjects. The provinces never saw them, and they knew little of the workaday life outside the capital. George III had his political faults and follies, but his few weeks at Cheltenham, soon followed by his annual summer sojourns at Weymouth, brought the Crown visibly nearer to the country's ordinary citizens.

Cheltenham's chances of growth were soon checked by the French Revolutionary War. The spa's fashionable life continued, but little was done for the town's architectural embellishment. Financial stringency and the lack of good transport lay behind the delay. Navigable water was then the best means whereby such things as coal and building timber could reach a growing town. But the scheme of 1792 for a canal from the Severn to Coombe Hill petered out at the former place. A project of 1810 for its continuance to Cheltenham and a scheme, of the same year, for a canal direct from Tewkesbury to the spa town came to nothing. Only when in 1811 a horse tramway linked Cheltenham with the timber-importing facilities of Gloucester Quay could all the factors of production be assembled on Cheltenham's building sites. The simply-designed, unadorned Royal Crescent had already been finished, giving those who lodged in it a charmingly un-impeded view across the meadows to the escarpment of the Cotswolds. Then after the Napoleonic War the town started to expand. Cambray Place and the simply-fronted terraces along the London road were all built by 1820; in another year the census showed that the population stood at about 13,300. By now the Montpellier Spa had commenced its operations, and in 1818 the charming Sherborne, or Imperial, Pump Room was taken in hand. The tree-lined Sherborne Walk which led to this little Ionic building gave the alignment for the Promenade. To understand the manner of Chelten-ham's growth, and the way in which the life of its visitors and residents was disposed, one must recall that Cheltenham, unlike Bath with its central, concentrated spa area, was a place where the mineral waters were tapped at several scattered places. So far the spa areas lay south of the High Street; in a few more years the spectacular northern develop-ment of Pittville was begun.

By now Cheltenham had become sure of its position as England's premier spa. It was significant, as one still sees along the Fosse Way in villages near Shepton Mallet, that the mileposts of a turnpike trust in northern Somerset gave the distance not to neighbouring Bath but to more distant Cheltenham. Where Cheltenham lagged was in its local government. Unlike Bath and Gloucester it was no ancient, well-established borough with a Mayor and Corporation. The Vestry, and the Paving Commissioners of 1786 who later, under Acts of 1806 and 1821, became known as the Town Commissioners, long served as the governing body of a growing town. Despite a strengthening of their position in 1852 they proved insufficient for their task. But Cheltenham did not, before 1876 when its people numbered over 40,000, become a municipal borough of the type one expects in so distinguished a town.*

The architecture of 'Regency' Cheltenham turned closely on the readily available materials. It also reflected the styles (bar pseudo-Egyptian) prevailing when it was built. Though Cotswold stone lay close at hand it was not used for the complete structure of many new buildings. It more often appeared as a facing over brick walls. Brickwork was seldom left exposed, though one sees it in the Manchester Hotel in Clarence Street and also, in a check pattern of red and yellow, in the poor quarter put up north of the High Street and west of Evesham road. More typically, the brick walls of Cheltenham's elegant terraces and villas were coated in front with creamy stucco to give the semblance of stone. Against such a background the delicate wrought ironwork of porches and balconies could best be seen, its patterns being exquisitely repeated as they cast their shadows on to the stucco behind them. At first, as in Cambray Place and the Royal Crescent, the style of Cheltenham's new buildings was the bald, almost stark, simplicity of 'Regency' at its least self-conscious. From those plain frontages one moved, overwhelmingly, to the scholarly purism of the Greek revival. Gothic, as it was used by the pre-ecclesiological architects of its revival, appeared in some Anglican churches and Nonconformist chapels. But other Nonconformist buildings, such as the Ebenezer and Wesley Chapels of 1812 and 1839, stayed within the tradition of plain frontages and classical porches. The pseudo-Indian entrance screen of the Market echoed Sezincote and tuned in with the town's Oriental connection. Yet Doric, Ionic, and Corinthian, as these orders had been known to the Greeks of the fifth and fourth centuries before Christ, conditioned and dominated the sophisticated Cheltenham scene.

Its Indian connection did more than most things to make Cheltenham a residential town. The waters were recommended for the liver and digestive complaints picked up on service in India. So soldiers and civil servants flocked, for residential retirement, to Cheltenham, and such topics as life in Calcutta or Madras, battles at Aliwal and Chillianwallah, Indiamen and ships' husbands, and the Company's Colleges at Addiscombe and Haileybury became familiar in local conversation. In a few more years the Mutiny caused intense anxiety, and much bereavement, among those who had settled in the town. One can never over-estimate the importance, for Cheltenham, of its close link with India. Educational needs, and the town's rise as a great place of schooling, flowed from its fame as a town of leisured residence, and of Evangelical piety under the

* The local government history of Cheltenham, and the steps whereby it became a borough, have been well told by Mrs Gwen Hart in *A History of Cheltenham*, 1965.

despotism of goodness' set up by its renowned rector Francis Close.

By 1840 the growth of 'Regency' Cheltenham was virtually complete. The town stood on the brink of new ventures, ushering in its placid Victorian phase. From details which now became available we can study the town's human pattern of 1841, the year which saw the first classes held in the Proprietary College.

Cheltenham's earliest Directory, brought out in 1800, mentioned lodging houses and listed Cheltenham's forty laundresses and 'clear starchers'. It added that there was 'no particular manufactory in the place and but little trade in the winter', and that 'the chief dependence of the inhabitants is on their lodgings and the business that is done with the Nobility and Gentry'. By and large the same was true in another forty years. The directories, and the details recorded in the Census of 1841, show that Cheltenham was still a town depending mainly on the services it could render its genteel visitors and residents. The Directory of 1840 mentions little manufacturing activity, though Charles Beddoe, a chemist and saucemaker, advertised his 'Wellington Sauce' from an original recipe which had helped to impart fame to the Iron Duke's table. A pianomaker named Binfield also advertised; he referred to good reports on his products which had been sent out to India and elsewhere in the tropics.

Cheltenham's population in 1841 was 31,411. Females outnumbered males by nearly 4,500, and nearly 20,000 of the inhabitants had been born outside Gloucestershire. More of its character is shown by the occupational details, and the facts gleaned from the house-by-house listing of those who dwelt in certain streets.

Most of the manual workers were in trades directly arising from the main character of the town. Exceptions, from older traditions, were the 100 men listed as brewers, maltsters and coopers, and the surprisingly large numbers of 40 farmers and graziers and 266 agricultural labourers. The 253 gardeners (out of 1,544 in the whole county, including Bristol) could be explained by the residents' numerous private gardens. The 393 laundry workers and washerwomen, the 487 boot-and-shoe makers, the 916 male and 3,599 female domestics, and the 1,074 people classed as dressmakers, milliners, hat and bonnetmakers, tailors, and stay or corsetmakers were the expected appanages of a genteel, leisured, community which included 616 'independent' males, and 1,877 women under the same heading. The building and decorating trade, employing 1,123 people, may have been a little down on a peak of a few years earlier. Also apparent were occupations natural in a town of invalids and 'carriage folk' which had also become a shopping and commercial centre for the country gentry who lived near it. Chemists and druggists numbered forty-eight. Cheltenham's three billiard-table makers were the only ones in Gloucestershire, and the town's coach-making trade, with its forty-seven employees, was larger than a town of Cheltenham's size would have supported normally. At the humblest level there were 794 'labourers'; we shall see more of them in a glance at some individual, ungenteel streets.

For workaday or artisan Cheltenham one had to look in the humble quarters lying north of the High Street. Sherborne and Sidney Streets were among them; more totally of the manual workers were the newly built streets and rows to the west, in the poor district of St Paul's parish. Albion Street and the zone between Winchcombe and High Streets contained many people in retail trade, some of Cheltenham's large contingent of cabinetmakers and French polishers, 'flymen' whose fly carriages were a facility additional to sedan or wheel chairs, basket and brush makers, a trunk maker and George Lewis the well-patronised sculptor and monumental mason. In the St Paul's areas in Cleveland, Albert and Townsend Streets, one had an even humbler community. Theodore Curtiss, a 'Mormonite preacher' from America, was unusual among his fellow residents in Cleveland Street; the rest included wheelwrights, bricklayers, blacksmiths, tailors, a carpenter, a plasterer and a baker. Albert Street housed similar people, with agricultural labourers, a coach painter and a pig dealer to broaden the picture. In Townsend Street a cattle dealer, a Town Missionary and a coal merchant dwelt near a laundress, a milliner and various tradesmen and artisans. More revealing are the details for Stanhope Street, and for Milsom Street which recalled its Bristol namesake in being wholly unlike Bath's smart street of the same name. Sixteen people, among them a rat-catcher, dwelt in the Stanhope Street house of a confectioner named Henry Sidney, while the other working people in the two streets included an umbrella maker, two sweep's climbing boys and a scale-beam maker. One also found a large Irish colony; fifty-three inhabitants of the two streets had been born in Ireland. Many were labourers, but two were musicians and not all the others were in unskilled callings. As many of the children were English-born their parents must have been immigrants from some years back, arrivals from before the vast famine rush of the later 1840s.

Victorian Cheltenham continued to blend spa and residential life. Its schools became so important that *Eruditio* joined *Salubritas* in the borough's first motto. The town got its railways, and the sculptural concerns of Boulton's and Martyn's were of interest for their craftsmanship. But there was no real hint, in the stable Anglo-Indian social pattern established by about 1900, of Cheltenham's eventual industrial prosperity. A prominent Victorian figure, picturesque in his background and in his foreign name, a man of solid worth and wide benevolence, was Charles Conrad Adolphus, the third holder of the Netherlands barony of du Bois, known to Cheltenham as the Baron de Ferrières. His grandfather had been a Colonel du Bois, of a Walloon family. He served in the Dutch army, fought under Napoleon in his Russian campaign of 1812, and lived on to serve the restored houses of Bourbon and Orange. His son, the second baron, married an English lady whose forbears had included the Huguenot family of de Ferrières; it was from her that he took the last of his surnames. The second baron came to live in England; it was in 1860, some years before his succession to the barony and his English naturalisation, that his son settled in Cheltenham. There he became a leading townsman, and served as Mayor. Later on, he was the borough's Liberal MP, but he found party politics uncongenial and irksome. It was as a generous host, as the organiser of social events, and as a benefactor that he best deserved to be remembered. He gave much to the town's churches, paid in part for the new Art Gallery, and left it his fine inherited collection of Dutch pictures.

In the first decades of this century Cheltenham saw few fundamental changes; one notes, however, that the 'spa' aspect of its life now slowly declined into insignificance. But by 1939 light industry had come. Wartime dispersal, and the vast growth of aircraft manufacture, much increased industrial activity in the whole of central Gloucestershire. Since 1945 Cheltenham's light industry has progressed apace; industrial workers, not

spa visitors or even wealthy residents, are now its economic mainstay. Industrial buildings do not, however, intrude into Cheltenham's gracious central townscape. Worse
damage seems possible from large office blocks, and the tall building being put up to
house much headquarters work of the Eagle Star Insurance Company will be far too
towering and unmannerly for the district of Bath Road and the College.

Modern Cheltenham thus blends light industry, education for far more than local
needs, and 'residential' life. It is also a fine centre for tourists (the number of attractive
places within fifty miles of it is amazing) and it has become an important junction point
in the country's motor-coach routes. The town's own transport pattern has changed
greatly; Cheltenham's railway stations are now down to the original one at Lansdown,
while private cars and other vehicles are expected to increase so much that the latest
traffic plan, put forward by the County Council, allows for the closing to traffic of the
Promenade and some other streets, and for a 'primary distributor' ring road whose
course has been sharply criticised; so too have some road widenings and demolitions
which would be needed were such a highway to cut through some attractive 'Regency'
zones. For the people of Cheltenham are more conscious than they were in late
Victorian times of the classical beauties of their pre-Victorian buildings. Early in March
1967 a public enquiry was held into the scheme; as I write its result is still awaited.

We see then that Cheltenham's livelihood has altered greatly, and that new developments may mean that its centre, as well as the outskirts, will change much in appearance.
Another great forward move has been in the town's cultural life. Arts Festivals are now
much in vogue, and in this respect Cheltenham was a bold pioneer. Its music festival,
well established as an important 'shop window' for contemporary British composers, has
now run annually for over twenty years. The literary festival followed close behind, and
the live theatre has seen a considerable rebirth in Cheltenham. Despite many changes
central Cheltenham is still immensely worth visiting, recalling the special character
which it built up soon after George I's accession, and until the early years of Queen
Victoria. Yet one also sees that its existence is at present less artificial and less precious
than it was in the town's characterful heyday as a resort for invalids, bucks and beaux,
and leisured Anglo-Indians. For in addition to its function as a place of residence, and
as a solace for its many visitors, Cheltenham has become prominent in the making
and producing of useful goods. It has thus come closer in spirit to the days of tobacco-
growing, or yarn-spinning for the clothiers of Stroud, and of the making of malt—which
it still produces as a part of its ancient brewing trade, flourishing, conspicuously as one
sees in its new headquarters block, in that workaday zone which parts sedate Pittville
from the ancient thoroughfare of the High Street.

Mediaeval Cheltenham; St Mary's from the south-west

Cheltenham had a church in Anglo-Saxon and early Norman days, but the present St Mary's was started about 1170. Its crossing piers, and some of its western end, are 'Transitional Norman', while early thirteenth century builders put up the lower part of the tower. In the fourteenth century that tower was heightened and got its graceful ribbed spire; one compares it with those at Leckhampton and Shurdington not far away.

The rest of the church was gradually rebuilt by 1400; the task was not finished before the time when 'Decorated' Gothic was yielding to 'Perpendicular'. Some windows well show the transition, and the church is distinguished for the high quality of its fourteenth century tracery. In the north transept the circular window, with its radiating curvilinear stonework, is a great rarity in a parish church. The pillars and arches of the nave are less outstanding, but the cruciform plan was kept. The vaulted north porch, on the side whence most mediaeval parishioners of Cheltenham came to church, is an attractive addition of the fifteenth century.

The monuments are both a human document and an interesting sculptural collection. Those of the early Stuart and Baroque periods, notably that of the Catholic Lady Dormer (d. 1678), commemorate families locally prominent before the rise of the spa. The long inscription to Captain Henry Skillicorne is the best source for his varied life. Others are to families, like the Hugheses, who developed the spa. Later still, one has those which recall visitors and residents whom Cheltenham's waters did not cure.

The Early Spa

Cheltenham's early spa days were visually modest. The first mineral spring was found in 1716; it is said that the unusual nature of the water bubbling up south of the Chelt was revealed by pigeons pecking at salt on the nearby ground. The birds got sculpturally honoured on the corners of the first Pump House, and feature in the borough arms. A proper well was soon sunk, and fenced to keep cattle away. The site of this 'Original' Well is now lost amid the buildings of the Ladies' College.

Systematic development came in 1738 when Captain Henry Skillicorne, son-in-law of William Mason who owned the first well, settled in Cheltenham and built the well's simple brick canopy. This Pump House, the first 'Long Room', and its larger, more elegant successor have disappeared. Regency Cheltenham showed little of the vernal, informal freshness of the little summer spa which had over six hundred visitors in 1740. The scene round the Original Well lives only in pictures, like that of George III politely quaffing his glass of Cheltenham's saline water.

A Georgian spa needed a Master of Ceremonies and elegant Assembly Rooms. Cheltenham had both by 1788. Simeon Moreau, son of an Army officer, became Master of Ceremonies in 1780, holding the post until his death in 1810. He spoke several languages, had moved 'in the circle of polite company', and in 1777 stood for a similar post in Bath. His energetic conduct did much for Cheltenham; it included social activity, the publication of guide books, and active sponsorship of the Paving and Improvement Act of 1786. Moreau supported the Assembly Rooms, built by Thomas Hughes and perhaps designed by Henry Holland, some distance from the Original Well and William Miller's competing suite. Their site made them more convenient for the High Street inns where visitors still had to stay.

CHELTENHAM

Representation of the Grand Ball Room

Beneath Skillicorne's simple little canopy, George III drinks the waters during his historic visit in 1788

His Majesty at Cheltenham Spa, being his last Likeness drawn.

Beavan's is one of several splendid chemists' advertisements of the year 1826

J. S. BEAVAN & Cº
Late Paytherus, Savory and Cº
Chemists and Apothecaries
TO THE ROYAL FAMILY;
114, High Street,
Cheltenham.

Simple late Georgian; Royal Crescent, finished c 1810

CAMBRAY PLACE

The earliest terraces of Cheltenham, such as the Royal Crescent, the rows of stone-fronted houses along the London road, and those in Cambray Place, were very simply fronted and lacked the architectural embellishments found in the town's slightly later buildings whose facades consciously expressed the Greek Revival taste. These simple buildings were, however, adorned with many of the wrought iron balconies and other items of ironwork which are the glory of Cheltenham. Along with the Royal Crescent, Cambray Place, which was finished by 1817, was one of the first terraces in the area south of the High Street. Now a quiet enclosure, it originally commanded a fine eastward view towards the Cotswolds.

Houses in Cambray Place, c 1817

21

These picturesque houses are in Lower Well Walk, which still shows a little of the alignment of the Wall Walk laid out in the 1740s. On the opposite page one sees the graceful Regency entrance which till recently led into the Original Brewery, and an engraving of one of Cheltenham's smaller brewing establishments

BREWERIES

The brewing and malting trade continued to flourish in Cheltenham after 1760, when Thomas Gardner, formerly a maltster, started the Original Brewery. Other and smaller brewing establishments were duly set up, and at least six are mentioned by historians of the town. The early years of the nineteenth century saw the building of the attractive entrance of Gardner's Brewery, and of the new facade of the Fleece Inn; these have now been pulled down to make way for other commercial developments. The Anchor Brewery charmingly represented the little country brewhouses of a now-vanished rural England.

1809 MAP

The Cheltenham map of 1809 shows the spa town still in the early stages of its physical growth, but with the beginnings of development which transformed it in the next thirty years. The Original Well stands half way up Well Walk, but the Montpellier Spa has now also been opened, and the map shows some other springs, such as the Orchard and Essex Wells, which never became important. The Royal Crescent is conspicuous to the south of High Street, while the Tramway from Gloucester (marked as the Rail Road) runs to its terminus near the Lower Turnpike and close to what soon became the site of the Gas Works. But most of Cheltenham is still confined to the High Street and to various streets running a short distance on each side of it. The Assembly Rooms, the Play House, the Market House, the Grammar School, and the Plough and Fleece Inns with their agricultural names, are prominently marked along its course.

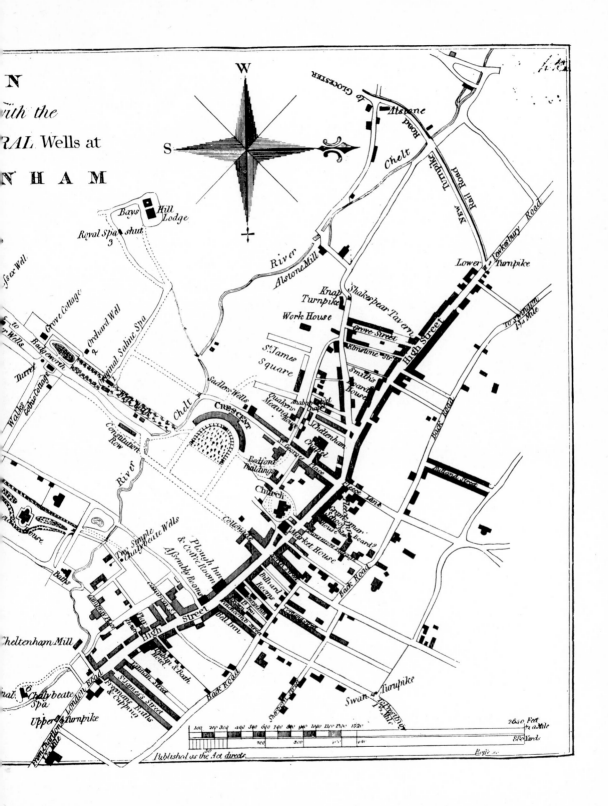

N

ith the

RAL Wells at

NHAM

W

S

Bays
Hill
Lodge

Royal Spa shut
3

Gloss Well

Grove Cottage

Orchard Well
2

to
Wells

Fadgworth

Turret

Cobra Cottage

Constitution
Row

River

Baths

Cheltenham Mill

Chalybeate
Spa

Upper Turnpike

London Road

To GLOUCESTER

Alstone

Chelt

River

Alstone Mill

Original Saline Spa

Sadlers Wells

CRESCENT

Two Simple
Chalybeate Wells

Plough Inn
& Card Room
Assembly Rooms

Colonnade

High   Street

Ball Inn

Bedford
Buildings

Church

Billiard
Rooms

New Turnpike

Rail Road

Knap
Turnpike

Work House

St James
Square

Quakers
Meeting house

anabaptist
Chapel

N Cheltenham
Chapel

Grove Place

Beese Lane

Market HOUSE

Shakespear Tavern

Grove Street

Alstone Street

Smiths
Board
House

Lower   Turnpike

High Street

Back Road

Sutton Street

Back Road

Crown Inn
Kitchen

Swan Turnpike

Swan Turnpike

to Swindon
1¼ Mile

2640 Feet
½ a Mile

880 Yards

100 200 300 400 500 600 700 800 900 1000 1100 1200

Published as the Act directs.

Roper sc.

25

Montpellier

The Pump Room of 1809

The first of Cheltenham's southerly areas to be tapped for its mineral water was the Montpellier estate. Its owners and developers were the Thompson family. In 1809 Henry Thompson built the first, modest wooden Pump Room; he soon followed with its colonnaded successor which may have influenced the somewhat similar Pump Room soon erected at Leamington. The spa buildings were approached, as usual in Cheltenham, along a charming, tree-lined walk. In the 1840s this was flanked by the famous Montpellier Walk, with its dainty little shops parted one from the other by Caryatid figures in the manner of the Erectheum at Athens and of the 'tribunes' projecting from St Pancras' church in London. The opportunity soon arose for the laying out of gardens and other walks, and for the development of the Lansdown district with fine terraces and villas.

Pearson Thompson, Henry Thompson's son, succeeded to his father's Montpellier estate. He was a vigorous, enterprising landlord; he and other local landowners were among the Commissioners named to carry out the Paving and Improvement Act of 1821. It was Pearson Thompson, in another four years, who gave his first major Cheltenham commission to the London architect whose name is specially, though not exclusively, linked with the town's more sophisticated phase of design and building. The architect concerned was that somewhat flamboyant figure John Buonarotti Papworth. His first important work for Thompson, setting a precedent for still greater building operations on the other side of Cheltenham, was the circular hall, or Rotunda, which in 1825 was added behind the existing Montpellier Pump Room to provide a more spacious and elegant drinking hall. Its interior had an obvious relationship with the Pantheon at Rome.

Pearson Thompson, Montpellier's main developer

Montpellier Colonnade and Rotunda

PAPWORTH

John Buonarotti Papworth had a full career before he first designed a building for erection in Cheltenham. He had produced many Gothic and classical designs. He had made numerous plans for 'rural residences' and for ornamental buildings in gardens and parks. On the strength of work for the King of Württemburg he styled himself 'Architect to the King of Württemburg'; he also made designs for the Pasha of Egypt and the Shah of Persia. He was an adept at furniture design and interior decoration. He knew much about dry rot and was a pioneer of plate glass. Though in general an eclectic he was, in Cheltenham, wholly an exponent of the classical revival.

Papworth's Cheltenham activities were hindered by the financial crisis of 1825 and by Pearson Thompson's consequent difficulties. His authentic Cheltenham buildings are few and he was, for the Gloucestershire spa, a less important architectural figure than the Woods had been in Bath. The Regent Hotel, first a large private villa, was his work, and his drawings in the library of the RIBA include a rough sketch of Royal Well Theatre. His most important building surviving in Cheltenham is the Montpellier Rotunda. He also made plans for the replacement, or complete transformation, of the slightly earlier 'Promenade Room' which adjoined it.

Where Papworth was more important for Cheltenham's beauty was in his conception of Lansdown—Montpellier as a systematically planned estate, resplendent with its terraces and crescents. The two-dimensional alignment of Lansdown Terrace and Lansdown Crescent was due to him. But most of the detailed work was left, when lodging and residential demands increased, to such local architects as the Jearrads.

From a drawing by J.W. Hands.

THE MONTPELLIER ROTUNDA CHELTENHAM.

J. B. Papworth, Archt.

Published by H. Davies Montpellier Library.

Montpellier Rotunda; the interior, as seen in the 1840s

The immediate neighbourhood of the Montpellier Spa needed more buildings than its Pump Room and its row of shops. Montpellier Terrace and the simple terrace row along Montpellier Spa Road were built and, when complete, enclosed the delightful open space of Montpellier Gardens which lay between the 'Rides and Walks' shown in Griffith's map of 1826. Among the ornamental buildings in this area none could have been more charming than the fanciful little pagoda in the Chinese manner, a late echo of the chinoiserie of mid-Georgian times. It could have served as a reminder of past days for those of the East India Company's pensioners who had sailed East of the Straits.

An elegant banking hall.
Montpellier Rotunda;
the interior as it is now

Montpellier;
the Chinese pagoda

Specially famous in Cheltenham are the Caryatid figures between the shops of Montpellier Walk. Of plaster, and armless like their mutilated prototypes in the Erectheum at Athens, they closely resemble Rossi's slightly earlier figures at St Pancras' Church in London

Balconies, a porch, and cast-iron, urn-tipped railings—these are typical elements in Cheltenham's great wealth of ornamental ironwork

Ironwork

In Cheltenham, as in some other towns where great growth occurred early last century, a major visual glory lies in the varied patterns and designs of the town's wrought ironwork. It is a choice embellishment of the architecture of streets and terraces, and to a lesser degree of individual villas. One also finds it in Bath (far less splendidly than in Cheltenham), in the Clifton district of Bristol, in Brighton and Leamington, and in the spa quarter and elsewhere in Gloucester. Wrought ironwork of this period can, indeed, appear on any houses built at this time; there are few more splendid displays of it than in the balconies of Avenue House in Wells. But in no town are the sheer quantity, and the average quality, of wrought ironwork better than in Cheltenham. Some balconies, in Lansdown Crescent for instance, are of cast iron.

The best of Cheltenham's wrought ironwork appears on the earlier terraces, with their simply-designed facades. It is also seen on later houses where the frontages are so plainly laid out and so sparsely adorned with such architectural features as mouldings, pediments, and pilasters as to emphasise the varied, delicate, at times assertive patterns of their wrought ironwork. Their ironwork in fact gives them a double decoration, for the patterns can be repeated, when the sun is out, on the stonework or stucco behind them. In later buildings, especially in those built soon before and soon after Queen Victoria's accession, the quality and delicacy of the ironwork decline into heavy coarseness.

Some of the finest of this 'Regency' ironwork in Cheltenham occurs in delicate little porches over the front doors of houses in some of the less spectacular streets. The rest of it is mostly at first-floor level, in hundreds of balconies. Some of these balconies are small, projecting in front of individual windows and meant for displaying flowers. Elsewhere, the balconies stretch from house to house, some being canopied and others plain. However designed and built they are part of that uniformity of composition which is the essence of classicism. Just as the idea of a Georgian terrace means the unifying, in one design, of several houses, so the balconies on such a terrace demand integrated design and uniformity of colour. It follows, as with the painted stucco, that the owners of all the houses should paint their balconies the same, in dark colours contrasting well with the stone-like creaminess of the background.

The patterns in Cheltenham's external ironwork vary widely. A few have Gothic references, some are florally romantic. But most idioms are of the Greek Revival; key patterns, anthemia, and 'Etruscan' mouldings are all in evidence. What still baffles students is the source of these designs. One assumes that the makers consulted pattern books, but I have never seen such a book which could have been a source for much ironwork in Cheltenham. L. N. Cottingham's *Smith's and Founder's Directory* of 1823 shows one rare anthemion design which appears in Columbia Place, but the artistic source for nearly all of Cheltenham's beautiful ironwork remains obscure.

Nor do we get much help on the forges and foundries where the components of these porches and balconies were made. Cheltenham itself, if one judges from its early Directories and the Census returns of 1841, seems not to have been the place of their manufacture. Advertisements in books refer to 'furnishing ironmongers'—tradesmen who would get stoves and kitchen ranges from the normal sources of supply. But they do not mention smiths who could have designed and wrought the ornamental ironwork. Only the receipted bills of the contractors who put up the local terraces and villas could conclusively tell us whence those builders got these ironwork items. Such papers may exist, but I have never seen any collections of this kind. Meanwhile, one would hazard the guess that the Black Country, via its canals, the Severn to Gloucester, and then the tramway to the 'artisan' district of Cheltenham, was the district whence this wrought ironwork came.

Balconies in a continuous run

Two more dainty little porches have hoods of differing types

More balconies display Cheltenham's wide variety of ironwork patterns

These canopied balconies face the London road

Ornamental ironwork in canopied balconies

Lansdown Terrace

The Lansdown district was developed to meet the needs of Cheltenham's growing army of permanent residents and of those visitors who patronised the Montpellier Spa. After 1827 it included, in Lansdown Place and Lansdown Road, the broad, tree-lined western highway which gave Cheltenham the finest of its approaches. Lansdown Place, Lansdown Terrace, and the long, cliff-like Lansdown Crescent with its paired Doric porches, are its most spectacular features. Lansdown Place is severely simple. Each house in Lansdown Terrace has an excellent blend of lower windows, a miniature Ionic temple effect like that in many Cheltenham porches, and two storeys of upper windows; this particular terrace was started, for its retired employees, by the East India Company. Lansdown Parade has a more modest elevation, with disproportionately large, well detailed Greek Doric porches. The later houses of Lansdown Road are aesthetically disappointing.

Though Papworth had prefigured the two-dimensional plan of Lansdown, the architects mainly responsible for its elevations late in the 1820s were the local brothers R. W. and C. Jearrad who designed more Cheltenham buildings than Papworth himself. They became the owners of the Montpellier and Imperial Spas, and of much of the Lansdown estate. The Gothic tower of Christ Church and the porticoed upper building of Cheltenham's first railway station were later additions to the scene.

Above, *Lansdown Crescent*   Below, *Lansdown Parade*

PERSONALITIES c 1825

This group of standing portraits shows some Cheltenham personalities of the 1820s. It is interesting for the light it throws on men's outdoor fashions of George IV's reign, and of the appearance of some of those then prominent in Cheltenham.

The gentlemen here grouped were all permanent residents in the spa town whose expansion was now fully under way. Four of them were among the Commissioners named to carry out the important Improvement Act of 1821. Pearson Thompson, the chief developer of the Montpellier estate, is at the front, in the middle of the picture. The short, stocky figure on the left, with his greatcoat descending nearly to his ankles, is Robert Capper, the owner of an estate named Marle Hill on the town's northern outskirts; he was prominent in Nonconformist and philanthropic circles and was the builder, in 1816, of the Countess of Huntingdon Chapel. To the right of Pearson Thompson, the tall, slim gentleman is the second Lord Ellenborough whose purchase of the de la Beres' old mansion at Southam made him a local resident; a few years later he became Governor General of India. Christopher Cole, on the extreme right, was prominent in various local activities, while General Capel, Colonel Watson, and Colonel Lennon represent the growing military element among those who now lived in Cheltenham.

This entertaining lithograph was brought out by the Worcester firm of Richard Dighton.

LIBRARIES

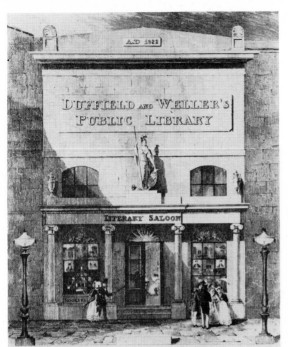

Public Libraries, and the newspaper rooms of such establishments, hardly existed in the days of the Georgian spas. Visitors and residents who wanted reading matter relied on their own books and their friends' private collections, or on circulating libraries and 'literary saloons'. Duffield and Weller's was, perhaps, the most elegant of these places in Cheltenham. The date on its facade is 1822; four years later S. Y. Griffith's *History of Cheltenham* lists five others. All six were in or near the High Street. The London and provincial newspapers could be seen, and periodicals and many serious books could be read. Circulating libraries were another side of these literary saloons' business. As in *The Bath of Sheridan* and *Jane Austen*, Cheltenham's more romantically-minded lady visitors could there satisfy their literary appetites.

The Market Arcade, 1823

THE INDIAN LINK

Mural monuments in the churches of Bath suggest that in the eighteenth century the spa on the Bristol Avon was a favoured retiring place for those who had 'made their pile' in the employment of the East India Company. But from about 1800 the tide turned towards Cheltenham, whose waters were more recommended for the long aftermath of tropical complaints. Cheltenham became *the* Anglo-Indian town. The retired soldiers, sailors, administrators, and medical men of 'John Company' flocked to live there; similar people continued to do so in the post-Mutiny phase. By late Victorian times Cheltenham's 'curry and colonels' image was deeply established. It continued until within the last two decades, and many day pupils at Cheltenham's schools were the children of those who had served in India. Only now, with no Indian Army and no Indian Civil Service, is this characterful element among Cheltenham's residents literally dying out.

Memorial tablets in Cheltenham's churches are a visible reminder of this great Indian connection. Captain Ashmead Pruen, of the Company's Marine, and of a family later well-known in Cheltenham, was buried at St Mary's in 1796. Holy Trinity Church, opened in 1822, has many 'Indian' murals. Those commemorated include, naval, army, and medical officers, the widow of a chaplain in Bombay, civil servants and the daughter of Colonel Boden who founded a Sanskrit professorship at Oxford. In Christ Church one has many soldiers and civil servants, and Lieutenant Colonel Kennedy who, as a young officer, had founded the summer settlement of Simla.

Strangely enough, Cheltenham's Indian connection found little architectural expression. The town's social buildings and villas displayed no equivalents to Sezincote, or to the Royal and Western Pavilions at Brighton. One building was, however, in a pseudo-Indian style. This was the arcade which screened the new Market from the High Street. The local architect, Edward Jenkins, designed it and it was finished in 1823.

ROYAL WELL TERRACE

Papworth's main employer in Cheltenham was Pearson Thompson. But the architect's drawings in London include a sketch for a building very similar to Royal Well Terrace which is one of the most handsome in the town. The sketch is dated July 1825, and with it are some ground-floor plans. It seems likely, when one notes the differences between Papworth's sketch and the slightly longer row which actually exists, that the design was rendered by someone else. As Robert Morris, who is mentioned on the drawings, was a builder he may himself have supervised the work. Yet the main credit for this fine frontage, with the Corinthian pilasters and half-columns of its first floor echoing Queen Square and Camden Crescent in Bath, and with its lack of a central feature recalling the Stone Building in Lincoln's Inn, belongs to Papworth.

The terrace now overlooks the Victorian Gothic entrance front of the Ladies' College. But when it was new its windows looked southwards, over gently-sloping gardens and fields, with the view framed to the left by the trees of Old Well Walk. Royal Well Terrace, though lying low beside the Chelt which flows behind it, was central and desirable. Yet in 1841 its inhabitants, including a surgeon, a 'chairman', three lodging house keepers, a Jewish broker, and an architect named Charles Thick, were not in Cheltenham's more exclusive sets which preferred to live further up hill.

The Promenade, looking north

PROMENADE TRANSFORMATION

The line of the Sherborne Walks has changed greatly, and not in all ways for the better, since the fine avenue of trees was planted up to the delightful little building of the Sherborne Spa. This Pump Room stood on part of the site now covered by the Queen's Hotel. The pump house itself was removed when the hotel was built. For nearly a century it stood, down the Promenade on its new site, which is now filled by a cinema of the 1930s.

In the 1820s and 1830s the Sherborne Walks (already known at their bottom end as the Promenade) were lined by their present buildings. The Chelt was covered over for an important stretch of its course. The mere existence of the fine terrace which now, with its later Ionic columns and pediment, houses the Municipal Offices, deprived the Royal Crescent of its pleasing eastward view. Continuous houses lined much of the Promenade's eastern side. Here too was the Greek Doric portico, like that of the 'Theseum' at Athens, of Cheltenham's short-lived Literary and Philosophical Institution. The upper part of the Promenade's eastern side was left as the open space now known as the Imperial Gardens. Terraces, and some fine villas, faced these gardens. Those buildings are the ones in the Promenade least sullied by what happened in the rest of the street.

Architecturally speaking, the tragedy of the Promenade was that, like Milsom Street in Bath, it became a fashionable shopping street. As this happened in the Victorian period it was an aesthetic disaster for the fine Grecian houses. Only when one looks above the shop fronts does one realise how good some of them were. Where the Promenade still scores is in the breadth of its pavements, and in its leafy beauty. It is much frequented for the high quality of its shops; for some aspects of the town's life it is the very heart of Cheltenham.

Cheltenham's finest single mansion was Thirlestaine House, dated 1823 and built by the wealthy Mr J. R. Scott. He seems to have been his own designer, drawing liberally on actual Greek examples. The stables were of unusual splendour and elegance. Picture galleries, flanking the mansion, were added by Lord Northwick

The Cheltenham Villa

Detached or semi-detached villas are as essential to Cheltenham's character as are its continuous terraces. In an age which developed a social prejudice in favour of separate houses, they became as popular as terraces. They were easier to design or adapt for individual tastes. They were built in the select areas—in Bayshill and Lansdown, at the top of the Promenade, in Pittville, and in the Tivoli district between Lansdown and the Park which was itself an area of sophisticated villadom.

Cheltenham villas vary much in size. Some are as large as small country mansions. Others are of middling size, while many are fairly small and are still suitable for single family living. Many are plain outside; in so far as the others display any style, almost all are 'Grecian'. Smaller villas, like some in Park Place, have porches whose column arrangement breaks the rules of Greek architectural design. To allow their front doors a dignified approach, particularly for ladies in wide skirts, they were built with their four columns not evenly spaced, as in actual Greek porticoes, but arranged in pairs on each side of their passageways. Here and there one spots a Gothic villa. Oriel House, sadly due for demolition, is one, while 9 Tivoli Road is another. Cheltenham is not the only English spa town to display these villas but here they rank as a special glory.

Brandon House, near the Park, and with a few Egyptian touches in its porch's decoration, is a particularly fine example. Its occupant, in 1845, was the Comtesse de Ponthieu. Archbishop Whately of Dublin was there in 1848, and it was later the home of Admiral Mackellar. The Ionic villa shown in Bayshill Road has a superb Corinthian neighbour; both are specimens of the Cheltenham villa at its best.

Ionic villa, Bayshill Road

S. W. Daukes's fine approach to the Park was never built as he designed it

The Queen's Hotel and the Imperial Gardens

HOTELS

It was long before visitors to England's spa towns were accommodated in the manner of our time. Hotels whose appointments recalled one's own town house or country mansion hardly existed. Traditional coaching inns, like the Plough at Cheltenham, were rebuilt in the Regency period, but their accommodation was still limited and many were rough and ready. So a move was made to build the large, fashionable hotels which became normal in such towns. The Regent at Leamington was a pioneer. So too, at Cheltenham, was the simply-fronted Clarence Hotel with its Ionic porch capped by the arms of the future Queen Adelaide who, as Duchess of Clarence, stayed there in 1827.

More ambitious was the great porticoed hotel which more than covered the site of the Imperial spa. William IV was alive when it started. By the time of its opening, in 1838, Victoria had succeeded, so the new hotel was called The Queen's. The architects were R. W. and C. Jearrad, and the feeling of the building was more Roman than Grecian; the Corinthian columns of the portico are said to derive from those of the Temple of Jupiter Stator in Rome. The hotel may have reminded some of its smart patrons of Palladian mansions built a century before. Its main architectural oddity lies in the elongation of its pillars and half-columns so that they rise through the height of three storeys. Such treatment was natural in a building which had to contain far more bedrooms than those in any private mansion.

In front of the Queen's, the pleasant Imperial Gardens were recently laid out, replacing the disused, hideous shell of the mid-Victorian Winter Garden.

THE ROYAL OLD WELL WALK
on the night of the
CENTENARY FETE.

CHELTENHAM AUG.T 8.TH 1838.

1838 CENTENARY

This gay early Victorian scene was staged in Old Well Walk on an August night in 1838—a few days after the opening of the Queen's Hotel. Numerous lights formed arches of gold and green, and people who turned out to celebrate were reminded of a cathedral nave. The centenary commemorated was not that of the spa's discovery; this had been marked, in 1816, when the Duke of Wellington opened the new Assembly Rooms. The event now celebrated had occurred in 1738, when Henry Skillicorne dug, lined and covered the Original Well.

The illuminated scene seemed one of unclouded celebration and gaiety. Yet the Royal, or Original, Well had for some time declined, losing favour to the competition of Montpellier and, to a lesser degree, of Pittville. In another ten years an effort was made, by the building of the imposing, classical Royal Well Music Hall, to revive the fortunes of the town's oldest spa. These endeavours had no lasting success; by the 1870s the dispensing of Cheltenham waters had ceased at the point where the little Gloucestershire town's fortunes had taken their great new turn.

D

JOSEPH PITT OF PITTVILLE by
WILLIAM MULREADY R.A. 1786-1863
Presented by his great-granddaughter
Mrs M Mayell

Self-made and humbly born, private banker and MP, Joseph Pitt (*left*) was among the most flamboyant of Cheltenham's personalities. He planned a new, sophisticated spa quarter at Pittville. His portrait, by William Mulready, is in Cheltenham's Art Gallery. His chosen architect was a young man named John Forbes (*above*). His background is obscure. His only other known Cheltenham building is St Paul's church, but papers at the College show that in 1842 he was still working in the town.

Pittville was the first spa area to be developed north of the High Street. Joseph Pitt obtained the land, as the rectory's lay impropriator, under the Act of 1801 which enclosed Cheltenham's Common Fields. In 1824 he planned its transformation. For his proposals one must consult the text, and the map, of Chapter X in Griffith's *History of Cheltenham*. The writer speaks of a 'new Town' whose rides and drives were to extend over six miles, and whose terraces and villas were to comprise a superb new quarter. Those which exist are splendid, but Pittville was to have contained many more. The year 1825, disastrous for private bankers and venturers in property, checked Pitt's ambition, and the actuality is a mere fragment of his dream. Many of the villas are later, mid-Victorian Renaissance and not Grecian. One may, however, rejoice that the lake and its two delicate little bridges were achieved, and that in the Pump Room one has the finest specifically 'spa' structure in England.

Pittville Pump Room rises nobly above the gentle slope up from the lake, proving Forbes to have been an excellent handler of the Grecian style. Its design combines, and in an improving way unifies, the elements of a colonnade and of a dome found in the Pump Room at Montpellier. Forbes' Ionic order was modelled on that of the little temple by the Ilissus at Athens. Statues of Aesculapius, Hippocrates and Hygeia were made for the parapet by Gahagan of Bath. Their recent replacements are by Cheltenham carvers (see page 94).

PITTVILLE PUMP ROOM

Pittville's Pump Room was started in 1825 and finished, for some £90,000, in 1830; the Duke of Wellington paid some visits to the building site. The interior makes a scene of graceful classic splendour. The Ionic columns lead the eye upwards to the gallery and the rosettes of the coffered dome. Downstairs, the curved recess has a set of columns to enshrine the restored fountain whence Cheltenham waters are still dispensed.

Pittville Pump Room's revival is one of modern Cheltenham's happier stories. Originally it never prospered, and in 1889 the Corporation bought it. In the late war it was used for storage and for quartering troops. Its condition was so parlous, and dry rot was so bad, that its survival once seemed doubtful. But its great value was fortunately appreciated, and large sums were raised for its restoration. Its structural rescue and tasteful redecoration were started. In 1960 the present Duke of Wellington opened the building. Now again it serves Cheltenham, being full of life and activity. It houses some events in the annual Music Festivals, and is in demand for social occasions. Its light, airy upper rooms accommodate the architectural school of the Gloucestershire College of Art, whose own new buildings lie close at hand.

PITTVILLE LAKES

The beauties of Pittville do not all lie in the architectural graces of its Pump Room, its terraces and its Grecian villas. Any area of Regency urbanism also owed much to its trees, lawns, and flowers. Though the Pittville estate is only a fragment of its sponsor's dream, its natural beauty is as restfully attractive as are its stonework and stucco. First come the lawns, trees and shrubs between the Evesham road and the earlier houses. The tree-girt lakes then comprise the best sheets of artificial water in Cheltenham. The stream which feeds them is a tributary brook of the little river Swilgate which joins the Severn at Tewkesbury.

The lower lake once adorned the grounds of Marle Hill, on the ridge over which, since 1810, one has driven towards Bishop's Cleeve. This lake is now the boating lake and is the main adornment of a public park.

A picturesque event at Pittville was in 1866 when the lifeboat, to which Cheltenham people had subscribed, was ceremonially launched before going to its station at Burnham in Somerset. Great enthusiasm was shown in a town whose waterways gave few chances for nautical occasions.

Workaday Cheltenham

The spa town of squares, terraces, villas, and crescents was not only the place of resort and residence of its bucks and dandies, of genteel ladies and of those retired from India. The majority of its population supported the elegant, artificial life of Walks and Assembly Rooms, of drawing room parties and of fine silver, glass and china in well-furnished dining rooms. One had the domestic servants, by our standards unbelievably numerous. In 1841, when Census schedules gave a detailed picture of how Cheltenham's people were occupied, six servants lived in the Lansdown Place house of Admiral Sir Josiah Coghill. In the same terrace, six were employed by a retired Army officer, while Mr James Webster had five and a governess for his six children. Two male and six female servants were in one house in Lansdown Crescent, while six female domestics saw to the needs of two elderly Lansdown ladies named Martha and Margaret Lys. Francis Close, the Rector, was content with a staff of four. One need feel no surprise that there were over 4,500 domestic servants in Cheltenham.

So far as Cheltenham was a commercial or an industrial town, its working people were mostly in trades or crafts which had arisen since it had become a spa, and which served the demands of those who lived and lodged in Lansdown, Montpellier, or Pittville. The keepers of lodging houses were a large element in the population. In an age when the upper and middle classes placed special orders for most of their clothes and footwear, those who worked in the bespoke trades were a large body. Tailors, hat and bonnet makers, shoemakers, dressmakers, milliners, and stay and corsetmakers were numerous, and one hears also of their young apprentices. In a Directory of 1840 a nicely-engraved advertisement comes from an 'Embroidress to the Queen' who kept the 'Royal Berlin Repository'. Cabinetmakers, to produce and repair the furniture of Cheltenham's early Victorian homes, were much in evidence. Chemists and druggists were naturally abundant, and one combined his chemist's business with saucemaking. Brewing was a local industry having its roots before the town blossomed out as a spa. But the spacious wine vaults, like the 'Liverpool Vaults' here illustrated, met a demand which the new life of the town had much increased. Those who moved the casks and bottles, like those employed by the coachbuilders, made their living thanks to the changed character of Cheltenham since the discovery of its mineral waters. Beneath these craftsmen and small employers, and below those whose living came from horse-drawn transport, hundreds of ordinary labourers and their families teemed in the humblest streets run up in the poorer quarters.

Cheltenham's main 'artisan' areas were near Sherborne Street and Fairview Road, the north-western section forming St Paul's parish, and the southerly district intersected by such highways as Tivoli and Norwood Streets. The first named was the oldest. Not much of it appeared in the map of 1809, but it is fully shown in that of 1826. St Paul's was developed later, and became the least creditable part of Cheltenham. Here was the district of mean little streets north of the Gas Works, of the Gas Green Baptist Chapel, of the unimpressive Brunswick and Hanover Streets, of little houses faced in a chequer pattern of red and yellow brickwork. In 1848, as Mrs Hart has explained in her book on Cheltenham, an official enquiry had sharp things to say on 'the other Cheltenham' of filthy streets, of cheap, frousty doss houses for tramps, of back yard pig sties, and of the donkey carts of those who sifted the scavengers' rubbish. Water supplies and sewage were grossly defective. The narrow streets and close alleys of early Victorian slumdom were abundant; the scene was less attuned to Cheltenham's 'elegant' image than to the teeming, disease-ridden cellars and courts of contemporary Liverpool and Manchester.

The Liverpool Vaults
In Townsend Street; red and yellow brick

STATE CARRIAGE,
Built for Baron de Pontecarvo, a Portuguese Nobleman, at
GARRATTS. COACH MANUFACTORY.
HIGH STREET, CHELTENHAM.

Carriage building was long an important trade in Cheltenham. Above, from Griffith's advertisement of 1826, one has a specially splendid work of the firm of Garratt. Below, Miles's graceful Victorian landau relies on the firm's own patent 'Cee' spring

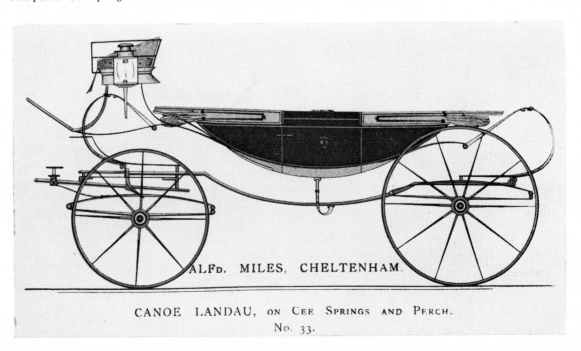

ALFd. MILES, CHELTENHAM.

CANOE LANDAU, ON CEE SPRINGS AND PERCH.
No. 33.

Transport

Coach and horse traffic at the London road turnpike

BY ROAD

All Cheltenham's pre-mechanical transport was by the roads and until these had been replaced or improved the town could not attract extra visitors or experience massive growth. Cheltenham's earliest approach roads were seldom direct. Isaac Taylor's Gloucestershire map of 1777 shows them curving and meandering between the neighbouring villages. Some, like the road towards Painswick, were hilly as well as devious. Even the turnpike roads were inconvenient and steep for any reasonably swift traffic.

The first road realigned was that from London, via Kilkenny and Dowdeswell. In 1785 its authorising Act of Parliament said that mineral waters had made Cheltenham 'a place of great resort', but warns that it would be better patronised were its communications, especially those from London, improved. The plan fitted in between the opening of the new Assembly Rooms and the Improvement Act of 1786; the Hugheses and Moreau, the Master of Ceremonies, were behind all three developments.

The next of Cheltenham's turnpikes taken in hand was that to Gloucester; most of the present road runs on the lines authorised in 1809. For the last stretch, and for much of its countryside course, the road ran alongside a new facility whose authorising Act got the Royal Assent on the same day in 1809. This was the horse-drawn tramway, by which coal and timber could come to Cheltenham from Gloucester Quay. One can still trace this tramway in the unusually wide pavement on the eastern side of Gloucester Road in Cheltenham.

A new road to Bishop's Cleeve, and so towards Evesham and elsewhere in the Midlands, was authorised in 1810. In another ten years an Act was passed for a new, direct, comparatively level road, by Shurdington, to the older Painswick and Bath road near Prinknash.

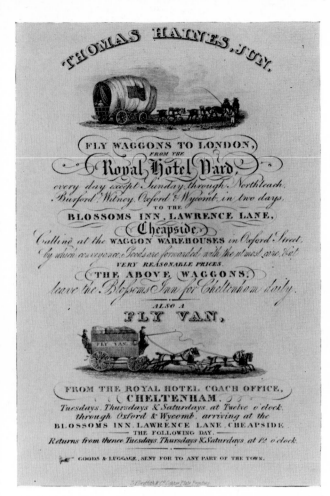

Fly waggon advertisement, 1826

Chaises and larger coaches first brought passengers to and from Cheltenham. For goods one still relied on the slow and cumbersome 'fly waggons', toiling along behind their teams of sturdy horses. The improved roads, with better surfaces and easier gradients, helped passengers more than freight. Canals, and for Cheltenham the tramway, were still the best carriers of heavy goods and large consignments.

In the porch of Christ Church

Lansdown station, as designed by S. W. Daukes

RAILWAYS

The railways duly became Cheltenham's main carriers and although steam traction was tried out on the tramway, railway competition soon overcame it. The railways bought the line in 1836 and abandoned it in 1859; by then ordinary railways were well established.

The first of Cheltenham's railways was the Birmingham & Gloucester, opened in 1844 with its Lansdown Station on the west of the town. The upper building had Daukes's dignified Greek Doric portico which has been insensitively demolished; now that Lansdown is Cheltenham's only station one finds it sadly shorn of the feature which gave it distinction. By 1847 the Great Western line from London, Swindon, and Stroud coincided, with outer rails to allow for two gauges, with the southerly stretch of the Birmingham & Gloucester; a branch ran on from near Lansdown to a terminal station at St James's. Its buildings were supposedly temporary, but fifty years passed before their 'dingy shedding' was replaced by the Italianiate passenger station only lately closed.

The delay in achieving Cheltenham's railway link with London partly arose from the possibility that a line might come in by some other route. The most ambitious scheme was that for the London, Oxford & Cheltenham Railway; its planned course was like that followed, between 1899 and 1906, by the line from Honeybourne with its its station at Malvern Road. The station for this railway was to extend along the whole six-hundred foot length of Townsend Street. Two drawings of 1847 show that it would have been a far more imposing station than any others in Cheltenham.

Cheltenham's railways are now terribly diminished. The two picturesque lines over the high Cotswolds have both disappeared. The stations at St James's and Malvern Road are shut. All trains from Birmingham, Bristol, or London run to the deep-set platforms at Lansdown.

London, Oxford & Cheltenham Railway; proposed Townsend Street station, by S. W. Daukes, 1847

London, Oxford & Cheltenham Railway; an alternative design, 1847

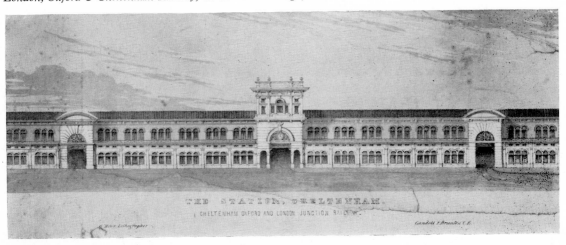

Tram No 21 on its way to a museum, 1965

PUBLIC TRANSPORT

Cheltenham's internal transport has been by varied methods. Private carriages were prominent at first. When Griffith wrote in 1826 they had been reinforced by sedan chairs, bath chairs, and horse-drawn 'fly carriages'; the drivers of the last named were apt to be an unruly set.

Electric trams eventually took over much of Cheltenham's public transport. The lines included a steeply-climbing line, up Cleeve Hill, to a terminus not far below the summit of the Winchcombe road. Cheltenham's trams have had their share of the nostalgic affection now bestowed on such transport relics as streetcars and paddlesteamers. The last one was recently renovated and sent to a transport museum. Motor omnibuses have now replaced the electric trams.

The private car has now ousted some of Cheltenham's public transport, and the town is beset by the general scourge of traffic congestion. In 1965 the Gloucestershire County Council published a Town Centre Plan for the future handling of traffic in central Cheltenham. Prominent items were the closing to vehicles of the Promenade, of much of the High Street, and of some short streets north of it, and the building of an inner ring road whose wide course would cause the demolition of much property. Much controversy has ensued, and in the early summer of 1967 Cheltenham awaited the result of a public local enquiry held by the Government.

Royal Statues

Cheltenham's statue of William IV, of plaster and by the sculptor Bossi, was set up in 1833 to commemorate the passing of the Reform Bill. Public statues of this King are very rare

Edward VII is more widely commemorated by public statues than William IV. This one in Cheltenham stresses philanthropic benevolence rather than regal majesty, being unusual in the informality of the King's dress

Places of Worship: Nineteenth Century

For over a century after the Reformation the old parish church of St Mary had Cheltenham's churchgoers to itself. Late in the seventeenth century the first Nonconformist congregations established themselves. Baptists and Quakers were early in the field, with an important Quaker townsman in William Mason who owned the site of the Original Well. The earliest chapels and meeting houses have all disappeared, and the oldest to survive are both north of the High Street. The late-Georgian Ebenezer Chapel, of 1812-13, was at first Methodist and was later used by Baptists, but is now a furniture store. North Place Chapel was built by Robert Capper of Marle Hill in 1816, blending 'churchwarden' Gothic windows and a Roman Doric porch, and became the local headquarters of the Countess of Huntingdon's Connection. The Church of England soon started its great expansion in Cheltenham, Grecianism and Gothic both appearing in its earliest buildings.

The first of Cheltenham's new churches was Holy Trinity, a daughter church of St Mary's which served the district north of the High Street. It was here, as a curate before he became Rector in 1826, that the young Evangelical clergyman Francis Close started his long ministry in Cheltenham. Holy Trinity was by G. A. Underwood, a carefully-balanced, essentially Georgian building in a somewhat weak and debased Gothic style. St James's in Suffolk Square, also Gothic and of more character, was started next by Edward Jenkins. He had trouble with his wide roof structure so that Papworth, an expert in such matters, was asked to finish the task. Papworth's own church in Cheltenham was St John's, boxlike and Grecian with two columns *in antis* beneath a turret.

Grecianism appeared again in St Paul's by Forbes, and in the admirable Cemetery Chapel (now a Mission hall) built in 1831 near the lower end of the town. Thereafter, the triumph of Gothic was almost complete. Christ Church soon followed. St Philip's, a much smaller building than its successor, came next; from then onwards one had the full tide of mid-Victorian Gothicism. John Middleton's churches of St Mark, All Saints', and Holy Apostles made him a local church architect of some note, while Ewan Christian's position as diocesan architect led him to design the gaunt, massive, unlovely church of St Matthew. The one exception to the Gothic trend had been the mock-Norman St Peter's. The Unitarian chapel, of 1844, had already given Cheltenham a taste of the same style.

By now the Nonconformists had also yielded to the Gothic tide. The Wesley Chapel of 1839 had, indeed, continued the late Georgian classical taste, with a Roman Doric porch now sheared away. But some other chapels were Gothic. The most striking, built in 1850-2 with two western towers in the cathedral manner, was the 'Decorated' Highbury Chapel of the Congregationalists. In another three years the Baptist Cambray Place Chapel displayed the Italian Romanesque which long remained popular among the Nonconformists.

Some Nonconformist chapels used in Cheltenham in the Victorian period succeeded earlier buildings. The same thing happened with the Roman Catholics. The original members of the congregation were refugees from the French Revolution; their priest, the Abbé César, had been a chaplain to Louis XVI. The first Masses were said in a private house, and then in a room in a hotel. The original chapel was finished in 1809. It was classical, and in 1817 a visiting priest called it 'neat and very chaste'. Later on, it was enlarged; the Census details of the Irish quarter round Milsom Street make its extension easy to understand. Then in the 1850s Charles Hansom's fully Gothic church, with its tall tower and spire, was built to replace it.

E

St John's, as designed by Papworth
North Place Chapel and an adjacent villa

MASONIC HALL

Cheltenham's Masonic Lodge was inaugurated in 1817, and many important local people soon belonged. A Hall was quickly needed, and the efforts to provide it gave the town one of its most unusual and distinguished buildings. It stands a little way north of the High Street, and being on a corner site presents two important exterior frontages. G. A. Underwood, its architect, himself a Mason, was well known in Cheltenham when he was asked to design this hall. His plans were approved by the Duke of Sussex, the brother of George IV who was Grand Master of the Masons in England, and the building was finished in 1823. Less conventionally Grecian than the hall which Wilkins designed for the Masons of Bath, the Cheltenham Masonic Hall is among the town's best architectural treasures. Though a few Egyptian decorative touches appear, the idiom of the building is mainly Roman classical, while the grouping of its masses is unconventional by the standards of antiquity. Much original furniture is still inside, and England must have few Masonic Halls of such architectural distinction.

Christ Church and Salem Baptist Chapel show the Gothic Revival as it was used, in its early stage, by two denominations in Cheltenham. Christ Church, built to serve the Lansdown area, was started in 1837 and opened in 1840. Its architects were the Jearrads; their masterly hilltop tower seems to owe something to those at the west end of Lincoln Cathedral. The plain interior was much altered, and given Roman Doric columns below its galleries in the 1880s. The picture above shows the church as it was when first opened; the Malvern Hills appear in the distance. Salem Chapel, in the middle of Cheltenham, dates from 1843-4. Its exterior effect is concentrated on the broad street facade, with its outstanding window in the 'Decorated' tradition.

St Peter's, by S. W. Daukes, 1847-9. Despite Francis Close's hostility to ecclesiology and the Cambridge Camden Society, this neo-Norman masterpiece is in the idiom used by that society in its famous restoration of the Round Church at Cambridge

The present St Gregory's was opened in 1857, and the tower and spire were finished two years later; they are much the best element in Charles Hansom's church. St Gregory's, dedicated to a great Benedictine saint, has always been served by monks of the Order of St Benedict

The Victorian Town

Lypiatt Terrace, a bizarre Italianate composition, symbolises much in Victorian Cheltenham. In its domestic architecture the town favoured Italian rather than Gothic conventions, so that the later villas in Pittville, Bayshill and near the College are Italianate, not Gothic, in their idiom. They may be less fantastic than Lypiatt Terrace, but there is no doubting their aesthetic allegiance. It was in churches, in educational buildings, and in such whimsical period pieces as the one-time Gas Offices at the bottom of Gloucester Road that Victorian Gothicism held sway.

Though people still came to Cheltenham to take its waters, the town's character as a place of residence, and of day and boarding education, became ever more established. The trades and crafts which supported a genteel upper middle class society continued to flourish, while industry was found in such concerns as Beetham's the manufacturing chemists, with their making of toilet goods and with their 'Larola' cream first appearing in 1886. Cheltenham still grew in size, and now at last its local government system caught up with its social standing and national repute. The Town Commissioners continued their work, but although in 1852 they were reorganised and given new powers the final solution was the grant, in 1876, of full Borough status. The succession of Cheltenham's mayors dates from that time.

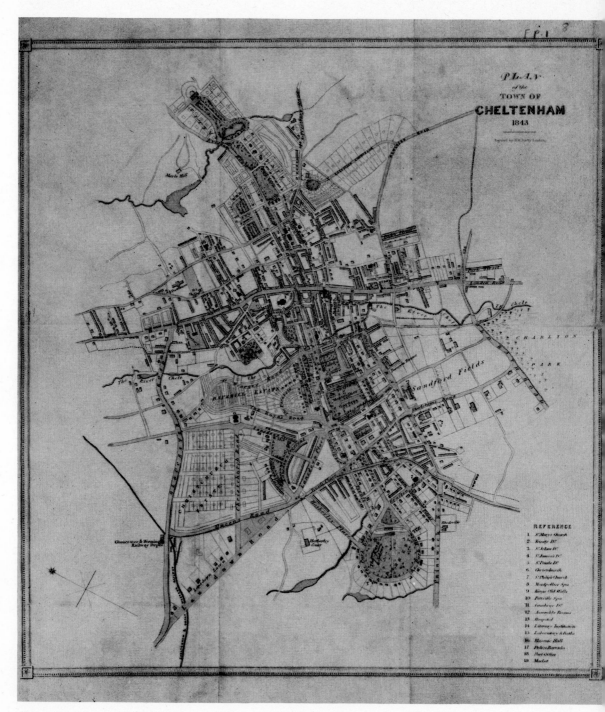

Henry Davies's map of Cheltenham, as it was in 1843, shows the 'Regency' town completely laid out and developed

Henry Davies's map, which was published in 1843, shows the 'Regency' development of Cheltenham virtually complete. It also includes some new items, such as the College and the Birmingham & Gloucester Railway with its station at Lansdown, which were among the new features added to the town at the very beginning of the Victorian period. St James's station, the terminus for London trains, is not, however, included, and only St Philip's, as it was first built, appears among Cheltenham's specifically Victorian churches.

Starting from the north, the Pittville Pump Room is at the very top of the map, and some of the houses on the Pittville estate had by now been built. But the line of Pittville Crescent is still unoccupied, and one can clearly see how far the Pittville development had fallen short of Joseph Pitt's ambitions, as these had been outlined in the map printed by Griffith in 1826. In the north-western quarter of the town St Paul's church and the workhouse had been built, and many of the humble streets in that part of Cheltenham stood complete. But other streets, in what later became the parish of St Peter, awaited their commencement.

The High Street, the parish church, the central streets, and the Promenade were in essence as we have them still. The ambitious project for Cambray Crescent, so prominent in Griffith's map of 1826, has been dropped and no longer appears. The Cambray Spa, a chalybeate spring with a little octagonal Gothic Pump House, is shown, with the number eleven, on the northern side of Oriel Terrace. In Bayshill, Parabola Road has been laid out, but only a few of its houses have been built. Much building has still to occur in that favoured upland tract. But less is shown of St George's Place, that particularly splendid terrace with a central Ionic portico and one at each end, than actually existed by 1843. The extensive Christ Church estate is shown as having been laid out for future building. But no development, in that precise manner, occurred, and the area was soon cut through by the Great Western Railway on its way from the Birmingham line to the new St James's station.

Not all of Montpellier Walk is marked on the map, but this was the year of its completion. Nor is the whole of Lansdown Parade included in a map which must have been prepared and edited a year or so before its actual issue.

The main feature shown in the southern part of Cheltenham is the Park estate. Its circular central space had for a short time contained zoological gardens. But it was by now laid out, with a lake and walks, as a garden of the more normal type. What is now, since the building of its late Victorian church, called St Stephen's Road is marked as Hatherley Place.

A picturesque figure in Cheltenham about 1850 was John Millbank, the dwarf muffin seller, who was only 3 feet 8 inches tall

Hexagonal mid-Victorian pillar boxes are a well-known aspect of Cheltenham's street furniture. Known as 'hexagonal Penfolds' from J. W. Penfold, their designer, they were made in 1866 by Cochrane, Grove & Co of Dudley. Cheltenham has more of them than any town outside London

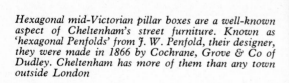

100 MILES IN A DAY.

EVERY MAN can have his own HORSE TO RIDE.

THE VELOCIPEDES manufactured by FLETCHER, at his Factory, Pittville Street, are made with the best forged iron and steel, finely wrought and tempered. They excel all others in workmanship and ease of propulsion, and not only much lighter but half the price of the London and Paris Machines.

Observe the Address:

SAMUEL FLETCHER,

Machinist, General Smith, Wireworker, &c.,

PITTVILLE STREET, CHELTENHAM.

The advertisements in the 'Cheltenham Royal Directory' of 1870-71 throw entertaining light on the commercial activities then pursued in the Spa and residential town

Umbrella Hospital.

W. CANDY,

Umbrella and Parasol Manufacturer,

81, WINCHCOMB STREET,

Opposite the Congregational Chapel, Cheltenham.

Walking Sticks of every description.

REPAIRS NEATLY AND EXPEDITIOUSLY EXECUTED.

This portrait of the Baron de Ferrières is in the panelling of the Art Gallery which was among his main benefactions to Cheltenham. One can imagine his amused contempt for the 'cold water and bread and butter philosophy of life'

GUSTAV HOLST
Composer of Music
Born in Cheltenham — 21st September 1874
Oil Painting by Bernard Munns
Presented to the Composer by subscribers
to the list at Festival 22nd March 1912, &
later given to the Cheltenham Art Gallery

The composer Gustav Holst was born at Cheltenham in 1874, and attended the Grammar School, where his father taught music. His grandfather had settled in the town about 1832; all three took pupils from Cheltenham's residential families and were active in its musical life

PROMENADE FOUNTAIN

The fountain near the top of the Promenade is a strangely Baroque ornament in so Grecian a town. It was installed when Victorian Gothicism was on the wane, with *beaux arts* influences gaining ground on a lingering neo-mediaevalism.

This Neptune fountain was added to Cheltenham's attractions in 1893. It was not presented as anyone's memorial, nor did it commemorate any particular event. One gathers from the local newspapers that the area in front of the re-erected Pump House of the old Imperial Spa had previously served as 'Salvation Army and Punch and Judy land'. The fountain's installation came as part of a general scheme to improve the Promenade. The idea came from Mr Hall who was then Borough Surveyor, and his design was much praised by the journal *Art Notes*. Hall's design was rendered, in Portland stone, by the local firm of Boulton. That famous Roman attraction, the Fontana di Trevi, is said to have inspired the designer, but I have yet to notice that Cheltenham's rates have been eased by the coins of those who desire, as well they may, to revisit Cheltenham.

Education

Early last century Cheltenham's educational facilities were divided between Pate's Grammar School, a National School of 1816 and one for poor children over the church porch, private academies and boarding schools, and the domestic endeavours of tutors and governesses. The Grammar School had fallen on evil days. Corpus Christi College, Oxford, which the founder had made the governing body, had imperfectly carried out its task. The charity's endowed income, swollen by the development of its Cheltenham property, was only in part applied to the school, and the sums made over took little account of great economic changes since Elizabethan times. Most of the boys were the headmaster's private pupils. For a few years the school actually closed. The vacuum thus caused, and its poor standing among middle-class residents who now demanded good local education, was duly filled by other schools.

In 1852 the Grammar School reopened, still in the Tudor building of 1576; a new schoolroom was built for the many pupils now attending. Among its Victorian head-masters was Henry Hayman, whose later dismissal from Rugby was the most lurid incident in that school's post-Arnold history. Reorganisation in the 1880s led to new buildings. The traditional site in the High Street was kept, and the new school was in the early Tudor Gothic widely associated with places of education. This building, along with the brewery entrance and the Fleece Hotel, was pulled down in 1967 to make way for modern shops.

THE GRAMMAR SCHOOL, CHELTENHAM.

The Grammar School building of 1887-9 was by the local architects Knight & Chatters. Its tower, appropriately enough, recalled the gate tower of Corpus Christi College, Oxford. The new buildings on Hester's Way, compact,

well thought out, and the best modern buildings in Cheltenham, are by Chamberlin, Powell & Bon of London. After extensive discussions between client and designer, they were built in 1963-5. Above, the main hall; below, the inner court and the library.

The most striking feature of the new Grammar School is the domed library at the southern end of the building. Its double stairway gives a most dignified effect, and its exterior recalls its designers' domed hall at New Hall, Cambridge

The original block of 1841-3

THE COLLEGE

Cheltenham College was a result of the town's Indian connection, of its residential character by 1841 when it was founded, of the Grammar School's temporary decay, and of social attitudes common among those who set the tone.

Among the founders a leading spirit was Captain Iredell, a retired officer of the Bombay Army; his sabre is still treasured in the College library. Francis Close, as one could have expected, strongly influenced the religious teaching, and the boys first worshipped in Christ Church.

Cheltenham College was originally 'Proprietary', with shareholders entitled to nominate pupils. As the College flourished the shares much appreciated. It was never well-endowed, and the first buildings (finished in 1843) were most economically put up. Many boys were prepared for Army entry, and for the East India Company's Colleges at Addiscombe and Haileybury. A great Army tradition and good scholastic standards were soon established.

The first classes were held in two terrace houses in Bayshill. But the Governors soon held a competition for some obviously 'educational' buildings. They chose the carefully symmetrical, early Tudor Gothic designs of James Wilson of Bath. The wide school-rooms of 'Big Classical' and 'Big Modern' flanked a central tower in a single, rectangular block. More classrooms, the original chapel, and its vaulted successor of 1891 were added later. Since 1945 these buildings on the Bath Road have gained by the addition to the College of the Grecian Thirlestaine House.

The photograph of the College staff dates from 1895, when the bearded Principal, Rev H. A. James, left for the headmastership of Rugby

The College Close during a County Cricket week

THE LADIES' COLLEGE

The origins of Cheltenham Ladies' College resembled those of the College for boys; the Rev William Dobson, the College's successful Principal from 1844 to 1859, was among its originators. Like the boys' College it was at first 'Proprietary', and the recruitment of a school originally for day girls alone was from middle-class residential families. Like the boys' College it did not start on its present site, and its stay in Cambray House was much longer than that of the other College in Bayshill. As in the College, real progress started under the second Principal, in whom the Ladies' College found an educational genius of the first rank. Miss Dorothea Beale came, in 1858, to a school of 69 pupils. When in 1906 she died she had over a thousand and had brought new life, and new horizons, to women's school and University education. She was the outstanding figure in Victorian Cheltenham. In size and reputation Cheltenham Ladies' College has remained in the highest rank.

In 1864 boarders joined the day girls who had previously been the sole pupils. By 1880 there were ten boarding houses, and the College had moved to the locally historic territory of the Original Well. The first classroom block, of churchlike appearance, was designed by John Middleton and was built between 1871 and 1873. Other buildings, all of them more or less fantastic Victorian Gothic, followed on the none too spacious site. The many-galleried Princess Hall was built in the 1890s on the site of the Royal Well Concert Hall.

The Old Hall as it was between 1873 and 1890 when a gallery was put in

Miss Dorothea Beale in the robes of an Honorary LL.D. of Edinburgh University, 1902. The award was an honour which crowned her great educational career

Late Victorian formality. The widowed Empress Frederick of Germany (Queen Victoria's daughter the Princess Royal) on her visit to the Ladies' College, 1897

A cookery class, about 1906

Francis Close; from a miniature of the 1820s

DEAN CLOSE SCHOOL

When in 1882 there was a plan to found an Evangelical Public School, the first idea was to site it at Clifton. The death, as Dean of Carlisle, of Francis Close prompted the sponsors to make it his memorial and to place it in Cheltenham. The first buildings, by an architect named Knight, were opened with three masters and twelve boys in 1886. The first headmaster, the Rev W. H. Flecker, the father of the poet James Elroy Flecker, was a man of real note, of Austrian Jewish stock but in Anglican Orders. He increased the school to over two hundred boys and was there for over forty years. The school's religious traditions have been maintained, and it has gained a great reputation for hockey. The first buildings and the chapel of the 1920s are of no special note, but some recent additions, by Mr Eric Cole, are more distinguished.

*Rev W. H. Flecker and his
original staff, 1886*

*The modern gymnasium,
by Eric Cole*

The original buildings, by S. W. Daukes, 1849

ST PAUL'S COLLEGE

For over a hundred years teacher training has been among Cheltenham's educational activities. The foundation of St Paul's College, when Anglican training Colleges were being started in many places, was part of a wider pattern. The College ranked as yet another of the achievements inspired, and firmly guided, by Francis Close.

The project for such a College, Evangelical in character and national in scope, was first mooted in 1845 at a meeting chaired by Close. After discussion with Lord Ashley (later the famous Earl of Shaftesbury) who was president of the Church of England Training Institution, the College started in 1847 in a rented house. In another two years the present College buildings were started in what was then Cheltenham's extreme north-western fringe. Their architect was S. W. Daukes. With their gate house, quadrangle and tower, and with their unsymmetrical design, they were typical of the 'ecclesiological' phase of Victorian Gothic. What was styled 'the female branch of the establishment' was housed, not far away, in a large Regency house in the High Street.

For many years St Paul's College, with St Mary's Hall housing its female trainees, remained co-educational. But after 1921 the women students had St Mary's College. The Park area became the site of their original building and of others frequently added. New and wider activities have also caused much alteration and renovation and a new brightness of colours on the original site. Of the totally new buildings the best is the chapel (see page 91, upper picture), built in 1909-10 and designed by Hodgson Fowler of Durham. It is a distinguished essay in the revived, scholarly Perpendicular style given new popularity by Bodley and other exponents of the 'Arts and Crafts' school. It is jointly used by the students of St Paul's and St Mary's.

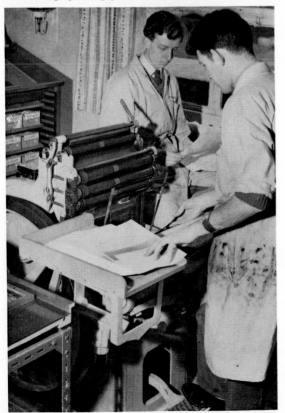

The College printing press

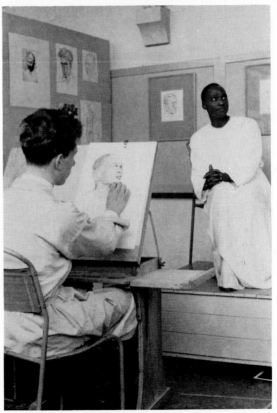

A student from Uganda models for an art class

Industry in Cheltenham

Despite its old brewing trade and its manufacture of toilet goods, and despite such craft trades as church monuments and woodwork, Cheltenham could scarcely, by 1900, be called an industrial town. The war of 1914-18 saw Cheltenham workers engaged on aircraft sub-contracts, and in the end on actual aeroplanes. What eventually caused the great change in its employment position was the rise in central Gloucestershire of aircraft manufacture, and the need for industrial dispersal felt during and before the second world war. Light industry, in a quiet revolution of the town's economy, has now, along with the Government Communications Headquarters, become a mainstay of the town's prosperity.

Early in the 1930s a few concerns maintained long-established traditions or opened up new fields of activity. The firm of Miles still worked in the coachbuilding trade. It had existed for some seventy years, and the founder's maternal forbears had been coachbuilders for many generations. The firm gained a leading position, captured the county trade, and won much export business in India, Malta, the United States, Australia and New Zealand. Mr Alfred Miles, long the head of the firm, also gathered much valuable material on Cheltenham's history; his volumes form a treasured collection in the Municipal Library. A more recent arrival, now the country's leading producer of a homely and delectable commodity, was the firm now well known for Tilley's crumpets. The member of the family who built up a small Cheltenham business to its present great output of crumpets, Scotch pancakes, and brandy snaps moved, some forty years ago, from the East Midlands where he already had a bakery concern.

The great new developments have been in light engineering. The first moves came in sympathy with the increased building of aircraft at Gloucester. The two towns, and the area between them, became more and more given over to making aircraft and their equipment. Then in the late 1930s some engineering firms moved from London to the supposedly safer Cheltenham district. Smith's Clocks, with their widely-spread factory at Bishop's Cleeve, were specially important; their workers, and those of the Dowty Group, contribute much to the area's prosperity.

Cheltenham's industry does little to mar the townscape, and the new factories are in any case on the outskirts, well away from the 'Regency' areas. Some recent factory and storage plants have arisen in a new trading estate off the Tewkesbury Road in the town's extreme north-western fringe. New office blocks can be a worse visual problem, and one of fourteen storeys now arising near the College is a serious menace to a skyline only punctuated, to date, by the towers and steeples of churches.

The firm of Boulton, well known for sculpture in churches and elsewhere, was started in London about 1838, with branches in Birmingham and Worcester. Some twenty years later Richard L. Boulton combined all its forces at Cheltenham; the town's equidistance from England's main commercial centres helped in his decision. Boulton's became the country's leading ecclesiastical sculptors with an astonishing output of statues, altar-pieces, pulpits and other church furnishings. They have rendered the designs of many prominent architects. Despite today's simpler tastes, they retain a considerable business.

BOULTON'S

Cheltenham College has some important sculpture executed by Boulton's. The great reredos in the chapel was among their largest commissions, while smaller carvings in the cloisters commemorate our present Queen's visit in 1951

*One of Boulton's craftsmen at work on the new statue of Hippocrates lately set up in the Pittville Pump Room;
that of Aesculapius is on the right (see page 52)*

MARTYN'S

The Cheltenham firm of Martyn's started, on a site in College Road, producing tombstones, church woodwork and a little wrought ironwork. About 1906 they moved to their present site near Lansdown Station; they then produced architectural metalwork, now prominent in their output. They also work on many furnishings for public builders and offices. Their Cheltenham employees number about five hundred.

Their reputation for fine woodwork gained Martyn's important aircraft sub-contracts in the first world war. By 1918 they produced complete aircraft. They carried out the early operations of what later became the Gloster Aircraft Company, and until 1928 aircraft work was done in their Cheltenham factory.

In the College Chapel; the memorial of the poet F. W. H. Myers

Work on aluminium windows for the South Bank Concert Hall

One of Martyn's craftsmen works on an urn for the new pulpit in St Paul's Cathedral

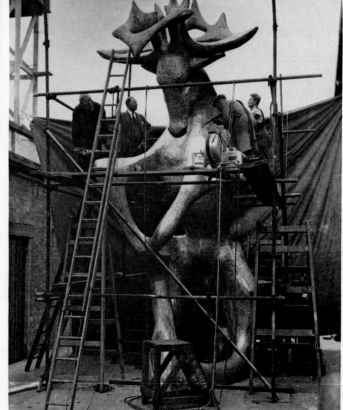

Martyn's works put finishing touches to the great aluminium figure set up, as a leading feature, in the newly-developed Stag Brewery site in London

DOWTY'S : THE BEGINNINGS

Cheltenham's industrial rise contains no more striking story of growth from minute beginnings to gianthood than that of the Dowty Group. Concerned at first with specialised aircraft components, the firm has now branched out to a far wider range of goods. The Group is still controlled by the man who set up his first little production workshop over thirty years ago.

Sir George Dowty started his engineering career in the south-west Midlands. Before setting up on his own he worked on the design staff of the Gloster Aircraft Company, building up a good reputation as an aeronautical engineer. He specialised in the design of undercarriages needed to support high landing speeds. In 1931 he started independently, carrying out his first orders in a workshop fitted out in a mews loft in Lansdown Terrace Lane. He soon moved to unambitious buildings, just north of the High Street, in Grosvenor Place South. His business gradually increased, with production orders booked after 1934. In 1935 support from A. W. Martyn, the chairman of a well-known local firm and founder of the Gloucestershire Aircraft Company, made possible Dowty's move to the mock-Gothic mansion of Arle Court, whose grounds allowed ample room for the great expansion soon caused by rearmament and war. Branch factories were set up in the United States and Canada, complete hydraulic control systems were designed and manufactured, and the wartime peak in Dowty Equipment's employees rose to three thousand.

Lansdown Terrace Lane; the original workshop

G

Arle Court and its factory buildings; a modern view

Arle Court; at work in a machine shop

Dowty's showroom has been fitted out to show the full range of the Group's products; hydraulic pit props are on the extreme left

DOWTY'S : THE POST-WAR STORY

Since 1945 Dowty's have continued to produce a wide, fascinating range of aircraft equipment, and in 1960 their amalgamation with the propellor-making concern of Rotol, with its large works near Staverton between Cheltenham and Gloucester, further increased their involvement in the aircraft industry. Diversification has also been a keynote of their post-war activities, and Sir George Dowty has keenly carried on the firm's policy of pursuing new ideas in engineering, and of devoting large resources to research and development work. The Dowty Group's products other than aircraft components include hydraulic pit props for use in coal mines, hydraulic buffers for the railways, and a considerable range of marine and electrical work.

Arle Court, with many new buildings added to those which stood at the end of the war, is now the centre of a wide, varied industrial empire, with many of its own establishments and several subsidiaries. Some ten thousand of its employees work in Gloucestershire, nearly half of them in the Dowty-Rotol factory at Staverton, with more at Tewkesbury and Ashchurch than at Arle. The firm is of great importance for the economy of all central Gloucestershire, and in particular for the prosperity of Cheltenham where Sir George started his first manufacturing endeavours. Dowty's have also done much to encourage the Cheltenham Festivals, and many other social and cultural ventures in their parent town.

Walker, Crossweller's factory is pleasantly sited in the modern district of Waddon

WALKER, CROSSWELLER

Like Smith's Clocks at Bishop's Cleeve, the firm of Walker, Crossweller was not of Cheltenham origins, but moved to the Gloucestershire town in 1937 from three small factories in the London area; their work was that of instrument engineers. In their unified, modern factory in the Whaddon district of Cheltenham they now specialise in the production of thermostatic mixing valves. They do much research into this aspect of engineering, and a large new laboratory, built specially for this purpose, was finished in 1966. Shower bath equipment, with special attention to the apparatus needed for blending the flow of hot and cold water, is another of their products, while recording instruments are made by a Walker, Crossweller subsidiary which operates in Cheltenham.

With some five hundred employees in Cheltenham, Walker, Crossweller's is one of the larger engineering concerns to have established itself, and to have grown to a considerable size, within the last thirty years which have seen such great changes in the town's economy.

TELEHOIST

With about 1,000 employees, Telehoist is Cheltenham's second largest industrial concern. They make various engineering products, and the bodies of trucks which use the hydraulic tipping gears for which they are well known. They now manufacture in India, thus reviving Cheltenham's Indian connection. Their fabricating shop, and a tipped truck, show something of Telehoist's activity

Sir John Barbirolli rehearses members of the Hallé Orchestra

A concert audience in the Music Festival of 1965

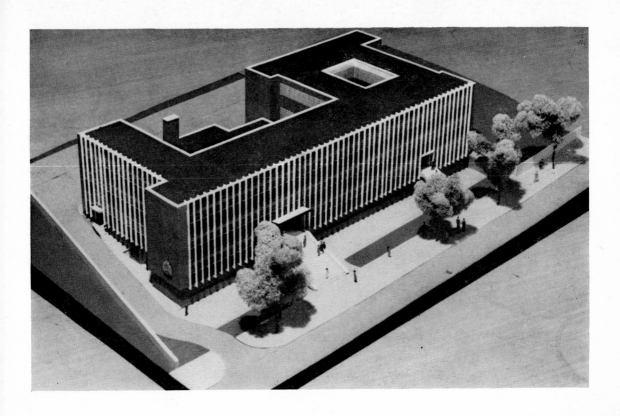

Cheltenham is not Gloucestershire's county town, but now contains some important 'county' buildings. The model shows the Central Magistrates' Court (with offices and a clinic) now nearly complete. Below, a home for the elderly in Charlton Kings

BOROUGH OF
CHELTENHAM

Scale 0   Mile

0   100   200   400   600   800   880 Yards

Railways ....
Main Roads ....
Municipal Borough Boundary ....
Ecclesiastical Districts ....

THE MAP IS DIVIDED INTO HALF MILE SQUARES

BASED UPON THE ORDNANCE SURVEY BY PERMISSION OF
THE CONTROLLER OF H.M. STATIONERY OFFICE,
WITH LOCAL REVISION TO DATE OF PUBLICATION.

This map of about 1960 shows the present extent of Cheltenham. On its left a most striking feature is the modern development in the district of Hester's (now Princess Elizabeth) Way. Cheltenham's railway system is shown still undiminished, and the site of the north-western trading estate appears as empty ground. But for the borough boundaries, and in most other ways, the map is up to date.

W. E. C. BIRD M.I.C.E., M.I.Mun.E., A.M.I.W.E.
BOROUGH AND WATER ENGINEER
CHELTENHAM

PRINTED IN GREAT BRITAIN BY W. & A. K. JOHNSTON & G. W. BACON LTD., EDINBURGH & LONDON.

105

Coronation Square forms a modern shopping piazza off Princess Elizabeth Way

Oriel House is among Cheltenham's better new office blocks; it is by Campbell Jones & Sons of London

A new building for an old trade; the new headquarters of West Country Breweries, by Gotch & Partners of Bristol, lies north of the High Street

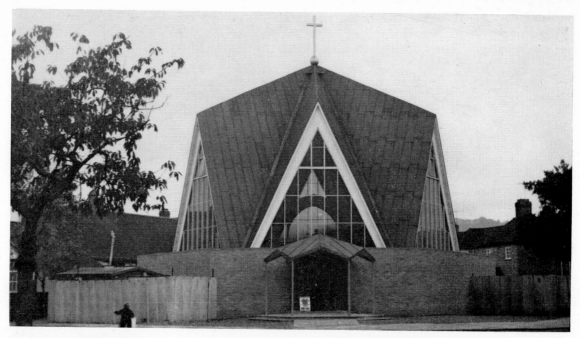

St Michael's (Anglican) by Stratton Davis & Yates of Gloucester

St Thomas More's (Roman Catholic) by Peter Falconer & Partners of Stroud

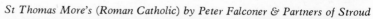

AUTHOR'S ACKNOWLEDGMENTS

Among the many people who have helped me over the information and advice needed in the preparation of such a book as this, I have specially to thank Mr H. G. Fletcher, FLA, Curator of the Municipal Library, Museum, and Art Gallery at Cheltenham, Mrs K. Pringle of the Library, Mr J. S. Bunt of the Museum, and other members of the staff both of the Library and of the Museum and Art Gallery. I have also had useful assistance from Mr G. A. M. Wilkinson, MBE, the Spa and Entertainments Manager, and from the Borough Planning Officer (Mr R. W. Hattersley), and members of his staff.

On the subject of ironwork I have had useful discussions with Mr F. C. Adey of the Gloucestershire College of Art, while Mr Peter Ryland, ARIBA, and others among my fellow members of the Cheltenham Society have provided useful suggestions and information. I have also to thank Mr Irvine Gray, MA, the County Archivist of Gloucestershire, and members of his staff, and the Departmental Record Officer, Post Office Records, GPO, London, EC1.

In the educational field I am grateful to Dr A. E. Bell, Headmaster of the Grammar School; Rev D. L. Graham, MA, Headmaster, Dean Close School; Mr E. L. Bradby, Principal, St Paul's College; Mr L. I. Davidson, MA, Librarian, the College; and Miss V. A. Hounsfield, MA, Librarian, the Ladies' College.

For information on individual business concerns I have had most helpful information from Sir George Dowty and Mr C. G. Irving of Dowty's, from Mr S. G. Larrard and Mr H. Burroughs on Martyn's, from Mr R. F. Coates on Boulton's, from Mr M. G. Lister of Telehoist, and from Mr C. N. Haslewood of Walker, Crossweller's. Mr J. Thomas, Secretary of the Gloucestershire Association of Boys' Clubs, has also helped me substantially over this aspect of Cheltenham's life.

B.D.G.L.
Bristol, September 1967

ACKNOWLEDGMENTS FOR ILLUSTRATIONS

(the numbers are those of pages)

By courtesy of the Corporation of Cheltenham (Library, Museum, and Art Gallery: photographs by S. F. Scorey, Cheltenham), 20a/b, 23a/b, 30b, 40, 41a/b, 42, 45b, 47b, 50, 56a, 57a/b, 59a, 61a/b, 72, 74a, 75a/b, 76, 77, 79; by courtesy of the Corporation of Cheltenham (Entertainments and Publicity Manager), 8, 31, 32, 36, 38, 43, 44, 48, 52, 53, 54, 63, 64, 102a/b; by courtesy of the Corporation of Cheltenham (Borough Planning Officer), 104-5; by courtesy of Mrs Gwen Hart (authoress of *A History of Cheltenham*) and the Leicester University Press (loan of the block), 24-5; by courtesy of the Vicar and Churchwardens, Christ Church, Cheltenham (loan of the block), 68a; by courtesy of Mr J. R. H. Jeens (photographs by S. F. Scorey), 49, 58; by courtesy of the Librarian and the Cheltonian Society, The College, 83, 84a; by courtesy of the Principal and the Librarian, Ladies' College, 85, 86, 87a/b; by courtesy of the Headmaster, Dean Close School, 88, 89a/b (loan of blocks); by courtesy of the Principal, St Paul's College, 90, 91a/b/c; by courtesy of R. L. Boulton & Sons Ltd, Cheltenham, 93a/b, 94; by courtesy of H. H. Martyn & Co Ltd, Cheltenham, 95a/b, 96a/b; by courtesy of Dowty Group Services Ltd, 97, 98a/b, 99; by courtesy of Walker, Crossweller & Co Ltd, 100; by courtesy of Telehoist Ltd, 101a/b; by courtesy of the Gloucestershire County Council (County Architect), 103a/b; by courtesy of Messrs B. T. Batsford Ltd, 19, 21a, 26, 27, 29, 45a, 46, 51, 66a/b, 67, 69, 71; by courtesy of British Railways (London Midland Region), 60; by courtesy of the Manager, Lloyd's Bank Ltd, Montpellier Branch, Cheltenham, 28, 30a; by courtesy of Cheltenham Newspaper Co, 62; by courtesy of Chamberlin, Powell & Bon, Architects, London, 80b, 81a/b, 82; by courtesy of Campbell Jones & Sons, Architects, London, 106b; by courtesy of Stratton Davis & Yates, Architects, Gloucester, 108a; by courtesy of Peter Falconer & Partners, Architects, Stroud, 108b; by courtesy of West Country Breweries and Bruce Perry Leedex, Bristol, 107; by courtesy of Mr Michael Hein-Hartmann, 34a/b/c, 35a/b/c, 37a/b/c; by courtesy of National Monuments Record, 18, 39b, 80a; photographs by courtesy of Eagle Photographs (Cheltenham) Ltd, *frontispiece*, 17, 21b, 22, 39a, 45a, 56b, 59b, 68b, 70, 74b, 78, 83, 84b, 106.